Melody Lines:
Fifty Poems

By Michael Sands

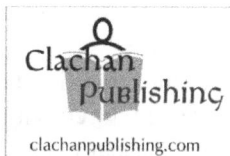

Clachan
Publishing
clachanpublishing.com

Melody Lines: Fifty Poems

By Michael Sands

6 Hillside Road, Ballycastle,
Glens of Antrim, Northern Ireland.

Email: clachanpublishing@outlook.com

Website: https://www.clachanbooks.com
ISBN — 978-1-909906-63-1

This edition published 2024.

Foreword

I began this project after thinking that some tunes in the Irish tradition do not always get a chance to tell their story. Often many tunes don't even have a name – *gan ainm* – or it has been forgotten or are referred to as 'do you know this one?' or 'what do you call that one?'

I asked my friends to suggest fifty random tune titles which came from the tradition already or were ones they had thought of themselves for a self composed tune.
I decided then that the title of the tune could lead me anywhere; I would not necessarily bind myself to what that the tune's title may suggest.

However, I did research some of the older tunes and their origin stories and some intrigued me so much I used those. For the original tunes I agreed that if the writer was happy to give me their inspiration for the tune I would stick reasonably close to that story.

In short order I had my volunteers both old and new.

What follows is the culmination of a lifetime in Irish Traditional Music and several months wondering why I ever started this madness in the first place!

The poems come in various shapes and sizes and hopefully a wide range of emotions are to be found within. I strongly encourage you to read them aloud in a crowded room with a glass of something to keep you warm.

I dedicate this work to my wife, Catherine and our children, Katie and Tóla.

Tá grá agam daoibh go deo.

the spoken note

When all aflow the swirling flutes
or uilleann pipes so true the sound.

Or concertinas drawing breath
filling lungs for hearts that pound

inside the chest, it may be true
that words are sometimes lost.

Without a song to set them free
silence claims too high a cost.

But maybe in the circle living
moments they can now devote

to tales and yarns handed down
and carried on the spoken note.

list of poems

1 - Hardiman the Fiddler
(Trad title)

I have given my time to these books,
in whose dusted covers a million lives
prolong. I have one only and dawn
is defining my road. Routine deprives

my inner voice but it waits no longer.
The sun is pouring into this new day
and I reach for the case long ignored.
As if from a cot I gather up and play

this fiddle. "Father can you hear me?"
I am unconvinced and lean my soul
into notes. They react as if called on
by strangers yet sing with each roll

and cut. The tunes from those years
in his old workshop where hung wood
to dry. The various parts of his process
on shelves, in chippings all have stood

me in good stead and I wonder at time
and duty. In my hand the bow aligns
with yesterday and tomorrow will see
courage displayed as it now combines

with liberty. Louder, I am regaining
those feelings, the old tradition passed
through generations swaggers my heart
and the reels come. I have amassed

harvests but locked them in caution.
I gather seeds and seek fertile ground
to throw them upon and there grow
a future where music will resound.

hardiman the fiddler – slip jig

Who was 'Hardiman The Fiddler'? A little research suggests that he is thought to have been James Hardiman, first librarian of Queen's College in Galway and author of Irish Minstrelsy, Or Bardic Remains, published in 1831. I imagine here the moment he decided to give up the day job.

2 - banish misfortune
(Trad title)

Tweets, taps, WhatsApp calls,
clicks and chat, Facebook posts,
make-do parades, Covid befalls
St Patrick. Impromptu toasts

from Cushendall to Tramore
twixt a crowd emerald dressed
watching dancers take the floor.
Hear musicians do the rest,

energy for leaps and bounds.
Flying feet land on stars,
the rhythms, ancient sounds
of tradition. Sad the bars,

meeting points for connection,
forlorn and of mirth denied.
Malevolent this infection
suspects not we are allied

to a benevolent madness;
an inheritance that maintains
those who have known sadness.
Its echo every heart contains

till courage cries, 'No more!
Resistance must now be heard
against a foe cold and sore
on Ireland if not all cured...

Swords aloft, raise your shield,
all misfortunes quickly banished.
Fight and win this battlefield
till blight from us all is vanished.'

banish misfortune – jig

One of the great tunes. During Covid the world changed and musicians struggled to find their place as everything we knew and loved was stopped.
This piece came from those very peculiar days.

3 - casey the whistler
(Trad title)

Of all the old farmers that ram ever knew
this one did what none other could do;
the favourite of lamb, of hogget and ewe
was Casey the Whistler from old Killaloe.

His Wellingtons gleamed the brightest of blue
with baler twine laced, each looked like a shoe.
His britches were fastened with old pony glue
and hadn't been off him since late forty two.

He strode to the field like Napoleon's heir,
his dog at his heels ran here and ran there.
The sheep in the distance did not have a care
till all of a sudden shrill notes took the air.

His finger and thumb pinched on his tongue,
he blew like a bomb had blown up in each lung.
The crowd stood in awe both old and young
in time tapped toes and along with him sung.

The sheep far beyond approached at great speed
then divided themselves into pairs as you'd need
for a set. Casey's change to a march decreed
they form in two lines as if all pre-agreed.

They 'Shoe'd the Donkey' between every gate,
next 'Siege'd of Ennis' all perfectly straight
although Casey by now with his cheeks in a state
blew on like the divil for fear he'd be bate.

The excitement was deadly, impatience grew
and as they all waited on cuds hard did chew,
until the winner amid cheers, baas and moos
was Casey the Whistler from old Killaloe.

casey the whistler - reel

I had never heard of this tune before but the title held its own promise. A celebration of the great skills some farmers must have to steer their flocks in the heat of competition.

4 - the mason's apron
(Trad title)

Around well worn boots the stones
lie scattered in a variety of sides,
smooth and rough. They slow collide
with precision, skill, skin and bones.

He foot-taps edges in rough audition
only stooping when unspoken lines
meet his eye. He grips hard to refine
their fitting till each is in a position

to rest eternal in front of the sun.
They will hear the moon's concerns
and witness how every star burns
holes into the night. When all done

his fingers sting in a dust coating.
Hard palms crash together like stags
in Kilkenny dusk, falling on tool bags.
His apron, fluttering and floating

from neck to knee is thus removed.
The leather of so many hours holds
all the secrets. In deliberate folds
he recalls the walls his father loved

and hears again old stories anew.
His work is every lesson learned,
his legacy is every second earned,
his memory set in stone holds true.

the mason's apron - reel

This is another of the great tunes from the tradition and comes with many settings. It has become something of a show stopper for those brave souls willing to attempt it. As this tune is handed down from one generation to the next the poem looks at the legacy of a different range of skills.

9

ſ - Rakish paddy
(Trad title)

He was a rogue, a scoundrel and a bit of a cad.
He was a charmer, a disarmer, a jack the lad.

The young ladies swooned wherever he'd go,
he was fond of the clamour and call don't you know.

And those of an age you'd think would know more,
evaded their husbands when he neared their door.

He relieved Lady Rose of one hundred pounds
after promising to 'freshen up her grounds.'

Lady Sylvia Smythe took the reddest of blushes
when he swore that he would 'prune all her bushes.'

Miss Joy Bosenquet went astray in the head
on his frequent assurance they'd soon be wed.

The English blue bloods offered little resistance
but all changed for him with some Irish persistence.

Moira O'Malley came not from that class
that spends all its days on its well pampered ass.

She knew little of wealth and little of jewels
and in her own mind she thought them all fools.

Mo (to her friends) it is said caught his eye
whilst waiting on lords and ladies so high.

Her long flowing locks as if touched by the sun
dazzled young Paddy, who said, "She is the one!"

He approached as she set spoons and a plate
for some boring buffoon barely fit to walk straight.

But she seeing him knew the stories and tales
of his playboy pursuits when on whiskey and ales.

Paddy enquired, "Your long day to console
would you care to come down to the pier for a stroll?"

"No harm I suppose," she replied to the rake.
"But I advise you quite strongly no liberties do take."

Says he, "Not at all, sure I'm gentle and kind."
Thought she, "Does he think I'm out of my mind?"

His temptation he found he could not dismiss
and at the edge of the pier he leaned in for a kiss.

She made to accept and the rogue closed his eyes,
she quick stepped to the left as arrived the surprise.

For he fell off the pier into evening's cool tide
and looking up saw her grin half a mile wide.

"Paddy, dear Paddy, you're in a bit of a state.
Soaked through and through and this our first date."

Back on dry land with his old ways recanted,
his lesson well learned taking women for granted.

It is said that by Moira he's obsessed to this day,
but if she has succumbed well, I just cannot say.

Rakish paddy – Reel

A 'rake' might be described as a bit of a lad, a hellraiser and a womaniser. Whoever the original Paddy was he must have been a colourful chap to put it mildly. I borrow some of those characteristics here but as you'll see he doesn't get his own way! This is dedicated to our great friends Paddy O'Hare and Máire Ní hír.

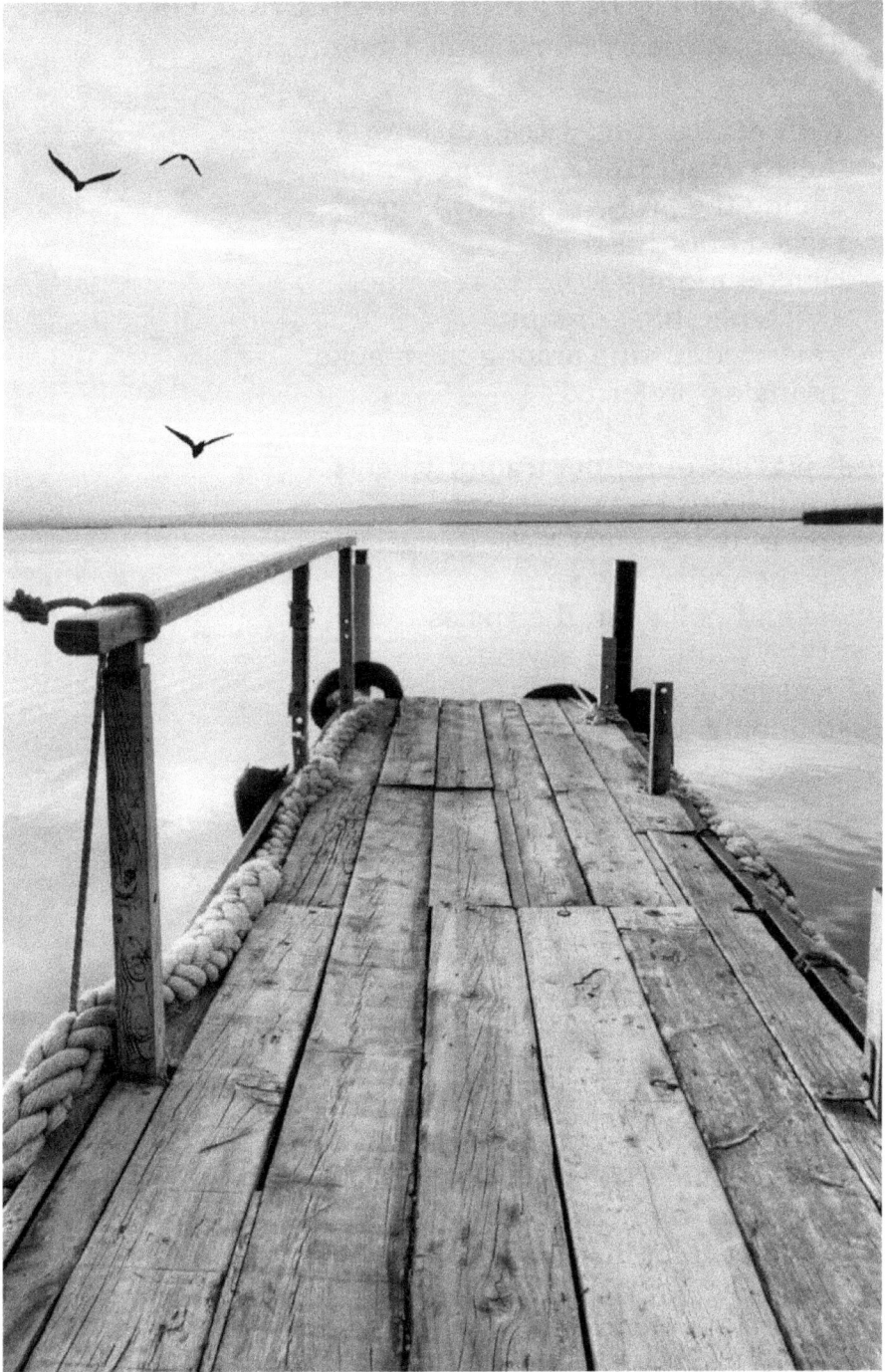

6 - ceol na móna (music of the turf)
(Original title by Marie Mhic Choinnigh)

Without a strum, a reed or bow,
there's music to be heard
among the green and purple grass,
ragged and unkempt.
Different kinds of notes resound
as if something dreamt
was freed to sing among the stacks,
drying as preferred.

It plays around the tractor wheels
grinding through the mud
and in the sounds of passengers
on the trailer swaying.
Jig and polkas in the voices
of the youngsters saying,
"Hide and seek" and "Catch me"
not doing what they should.

It shows itself in sandwiches
unwrapping near the fire,
in cups of tea and orange juice
after a morning's shift.
In the rhythms of the spade
this most humble gift
squelches in the puddles
and catches on the brier.

It's in the buzz of midges
and the flailing about ears.
It's in the creak of backs
and bags all aligned
It's in the journey home again
fatigue all entwined
with oh so many yarns
heard throughout the years.

ceol na móna – jig

I am delighted to have the handwritten original notation for this tune by Marie Mhic Choinnigh. I would often hear of her family days up on 'the moss' collecting the turf for winter warmth. I look here at the music contained in days like those.

7 - the musical priest
(Trad title)

The gathered settled in pews,
wondering what he would do?
They had heard yarns on the news,
but surely they couldn't be true.

The altar boy rang on his bell,
like Usain Bolt from the blue,
as fast as a bat out of hell,
from the sacristy swiftly he flew.

From under his cassock it came
a fiddle shining and bright
As soon as he said 'In the name'
the bow made the air come alight.

The Our Father and then Glory Be
the banjo he used to proclaim
Says Bernie to Seamus with glee
"Never will mass sound the same!"

Rarely before in that church
had these parishioners clapped
and no amount of research
could count the toes that had tapped.

Communion duly was shared
and as the recipients prayed
on the flute he played a slow air
as slowly the choir above swayed.

The accordion he saved for the end
and polkas ushered them out.
Arms stretched and knees did bend
Hup! they all loudly did shout.

Concertinas helped in Confession
with a bodhrán he did The Stations
Christenings became a succession
of sean nós dance celebrations.

Last I heard he was driving
a bus to the All-Ireland Fleadh
Attendance at mass was thriving
with each roaring Hallelujah!

the musical priest - reel

*A light hearted look at how mass could, and arguably should,
be!*

8 - splendid isolation
(Original title by Brendan McGlinchey)

Tides only turn because of the moon.
A fox may better assess the situation
thanks to its glow. Young lovers enjoy
its romance and bright peregrination.

The winner stands triumphant alone.
All eyes affix to fulfilled motivation
under the lights. He hoists the cup
accepting its glorious invitation.

The old king there 'neath his crown
meets destiny at his coronation.
Robed and regal he considers how
the battle ended in such celebration.

On the peak she inhales as deeply
as lungs allow. Below, a variation
of heights reinforce her wondrous
effort. Victory comes in elevation.

McGlinchey steers his bow around
old roads. His skill is the placation
of time and tone. He too contemplates
his masterpiece...in splendid isolation.

splendid isolation - Reel

Certain tunes in the playing tap into the 'other', a place between worlds where your spirit is guided by the notes to explore and experience something altogether different. This tune is truly one such.

9 - The cat rambles to the child's saucepan
(Trad title)

In moments when darkness held sway
before it retreated as came light of day,
did pad along among leaves and bushes
through the long grass, thistles and rushes
a most efficient and remarkable cat.

From whence it came no one quite knew
and no one suspected what it could do
except for a child no more than five
who with good luck seemed to contrive
as he waited with bare feet on the mat.

First meetings held sometime before
as just around dawn down to the door
the lad with a saucepan did happily go
and wait on his friend come rain, or come snow,
and magically they'd have a chat.

"Ah my dear cat, I have milk to the brim
in my newly made saucepan, shiny and trim.
An old 'tinker man' so adept were his skills
designed it for me then off to the hills
and unknown he went just like that."

"'Tis well I knew that traveller man,
his fine white pony and bright caravan.
My master he was and a-hunting I'd go
in the hours before day teeth I would show
to a rabbit or bird or vole or a rat.

We lived many days here do you see?
But a week is a month for one such as he.
The call of the road proved much too loud
I returned to tracks in the mud ploughed
and the grass all around it was flat.

He fed me each day right at this spot
Perhaps he felt sorry, perhaps he did not.
But if you agree here I shall ramble
and on your kind heart daily I'll gamble..."
"I'll be here," said the child to the cat.

the cat rambles to the child's saucepan - slide

A poetic title if ever there was...

10 - i buried my wife and danced on her grave
(Trad title)

How we ever got wed is a mystery still
sure I wake up at night feeling quite ill.
For there to my left with her stubbly chin
she lies like Titanic, ice getting in.

On my third finger a gold wedding ring,
says I, 'Holy God, that's a frightening thing.'
Then she would stir, looking over my way,
and hit the spittoon with a mouthful of spray.

Sure I had an oul' cock, the lad did his best,
servicing hens with his pointy out chest.
Till one slow afternoon believe it or not
she rung his wee neck, threw him in the pot.

Then was the time I only went for the one,
she sent in the priest, he says to me "Son,
your wife is in bed and your duties are clear."
says I, "Why the hell do you think I'm in here?!"

Away to my work, says I, "Where's me piece?"
"Houl' on," says she and spread on it grease.
The lard oozed right in, through to the crust
says I, "Must I eat it?" Says she. "Aye ye must!"

And there was meself and the match on TV,
says she, "Ye want coffee or a big mug of tea?"
"Aye with two sugars and a wee drop of malt."
But instead of two sugars she added in salt!

Nothing's ever tidy and nothing is clean,
she's the laziest hallion that ever was seen.
She complains all the time, never heard worse
"'Tis often I'm thinking, "Have I been cursed?"

But the camel's back broke when in a bad mood
she stabbed my bodhrán and splintered the wood.
Says I "Ye oul crone you'll pay for that crime."
Says she, "Y'oul ejit, ye could never keep time!"

"Ye boiled my oul' cock and bursted my drum.
Tonight ye are heading for old kingdom come.
I'm saying it now you will not be missed!"
And quick gave her neck an incredible twist!

I know just the place for an oul' weed like you,
six foot beneath that old rendezvous.
Where young ones still go down near the shore,
Murphy's síbín and its grand wooden floor.

I wrapped her oul shape, 'twas a terrible strain
then winched it aloft with a pulley and chain.
Next with the forklift I did her convey
down to the wee house next sea and spray.

I dug like a mole, best part of the night
then filled in the hole till all looked alright.
I replaced the old floorboards covered in sweat,
tomorrow night's céili will be the best yet.

Rolling in from the tavern the moon all aglow,
up sparked the fiddle with a hup! and yahoe!
Down came me feet and me heels mighty close
atop on the tomb of that merciless dose.

Sure I leapt like a salmon just off the hook,
slipping and sliding as the old rafters shook.
Had anyone asked why I felt so brave...
I buried my wife and danced on her grave.

i buried my wife and danced on her grave – jig

Again an intriguing title which just begs so many questions! I hope I've answered some of them.

11 - the earl's chair
(Trad title)

Their conversation responds to the tune
as seeds might when watered. They soak
the goodness of it into them like June
shone grass. "I'm telling you it was oak,"

says Tóla, content in the knowing.
"And I'm telling you you're wrong," replies
Dónal, struggling to hold his growing
frustration. "The tree beneath Irish skies

used for chairs was ash, no doubt at all."
A long exhalation from Tóla prepares
the ground. "I'd say you missed the call
for school most days." Dónal tears

into his pint almost chewing the tar-black
of it. "I was there enough to understand
that it was made of ash." From the back
of the bar reels are driven on by the band.

Amid their debate are forced out of them
roars of delight from deep in their guts.
They are hewn from years like shining gems
and glow in their passion. Energy cuts

the room into pieces and quickly remakes.
"Honest to God the Earl's Chair was grown,
cut and shaped from oak." Tóla intakes
a breath happy the winning blow is thrown.

"Is it your round?" asks Dónal, swirling
the dregs and pointing at his bereft glass.
"It is," says Tóla just as the whirling
subsides.
"Great tune."
"Aye."
 "Oak...your ass!"

the earl's chair – reel

Ash or Oak? I wouldn't mind really as long as I got sitting down. This tune has a grandness about it, fit for any earl.

12 - sean sa cheo (john in the fog)
(Trad title)

Suddenly lost he wondered where
the world had gone. "Can it be
an old stray sod does now prepare
my lonely and lost eternity?"

(If perhaps you are unaware,
the outcome of this situation
can lead to madness sad and rare.
Alas poor Sean faced damnation).

In cool and late midsummer air
he stood adrift among the glens
where he played without a care
with his sisters and their friends.

What he would give for faces fair,
familiar branches, hedge or tree.
Clouds to add to this nightmare
had come to earth for sanctuary.

Fingers raked all through his hair
"How many hours more must see
me trek the hills in such despair?"
Till came on the breeze a melody!

Every note shot up like a flare
and lit the skies above his head.
Heart ablaze he upward stared,
"This night shall not see me dead."

In the distance burning there
a light to buoy his rising hope.
He hauled himself into repair
grasping thistles just like rope.

28

He spied his daughter in her chair
playing her fiddle oh so well.
He entered gasping, "Darling fair
You've saved me from a fairy spell."

sean sa cheo - reel

*A great session reel here often to be heard at the end of a set
when the afterburners are at full tilt. I first heard of the 'stray
sod' from my granny Bridie Sands who recalled its confusing
effects to her enchanted audience.*

13 - Tripping up the Stairs
(Trad title)

Who is your man with the knees all folded
(his ears peeled back as if well scolded)?
His hair as if from a gale 'twas moulded?
Sure it's Tripping, up the stairs.

Who is the lad with the eyes of a stallion
(wide and wild like a bronze medallion)?
The only word you could use is hallion...
Sure it's Tripping, up the stairs

Who else has teeth as white as the snow
And chews like a bull all day as slow?
How it's all done his gums do not know.
Sure it's Tripping, up the stairs

Who else has legs like straw in a nest
And a back by work ne'er put to the test
and yet by money he's surely been blessed?
Sure it's Tripping, up the stairs

Of who should young ladies always beware
and him with the moves of old Fred Astaire
dancing at ceilidhs from Dublin to Clare?
Sure it's Tripping, up the stairs

Keep an eye for the rogue when on a spree.
Listen out for a creak and a sneaky tee-hee.
The very last person you want it to be?
Sure it's Tripping, up the stairs

Tripping up the Stairs - jig

This tune has definitely stood the test of time and will still be heard downstairs in most sessions.

14 - seanamhac tube station
(Original title by John Carty)

"It's all hustle and bustle here you know.
London rarely hears a minute's quiet.
There's an unsubtle din wherever you go.
Sure a bit of calm, you couldn't buy it.

I would say you would feel odd in a field.
After concrete you would sink in the sod
eh?" The boy stands up and is revealed
his years. "Da," he says, "honest to God,

you're some craic." Divilment calls them
and they prepare to go out across town.
"If you get a minute amid the mayhem
play the new one you just wrote down."

"Seanamhac?" "Indeed, Connaught abú!
Many's a day footing turf, building stacks
with your uncles. Having the 'tay' near two
and watching the wheels leaving tracks

like wet railway lines." Their usual seat
awaits, protected as if by a wizard's spell.
They settle around. Company complete
the magic begins amid the notes of well

known sets. He subtly nods as if to say
'this is your moment lad,' then leans
back into expectation. "I'm going to play
something new," knowing what it means

to his father. "Sometimes a tube station
is calmness in the storm. They bring
back yarns from the west." Incantation
introduced and in good order each string

+releases the work and captures the crew.
"Was that your own?" They ask as he ends.
"'Tis aye, one for the old country and new,
keeps me in tune with family and friends."

seanamhac tube station - jig

It is uncommon for a tune to bed itself into the tradition so completely as this one. It is, as they say, all about the groove. Mostly played as two-parter but there is an infrequent third should you care to look for it. I am delighted to have received the inspiration for the tune from John Carty himself and the poem is my interpretation of that.

♪ - mayor harrison's fedora
(Trad title)

Her name was Elora, a pretty senora
from down town Chicago or so it was said.
Her dad (a milliner) he did instill in her
a love of old hats, battered and frayed.

She sorted his shop from bottom to top
all manner of Trilby out on display.
With bright sturdy caps for elegant chaps
and lots for ladies passing that way.

One summer's morn, tattered and torn
her uncle, the mayor, set down his hat.
"This will not do. I need something new
befitting the office of an old bureaucrat."

"You see dear niece, he's chief of police
O'Neill his name, he's mad for the tunes.
Our meeting's at four and if I to his door
arrive with no hat my name is in ruins."

She studied his head which often they said
was a bit like an egg but much overcooked.
He went to each shelf all unsure of himself
while she thereupon expertly looked.

"Dear uncle," said she, "do you trust in me?
Father has trained me since I was small."
"Yes dear Elora." "Well, wear this fedora."
He departed the shop feeling ten feet tall.

The rendezvous followed, whiskey was swallowed
O'Neill and the mayor his collection agreed.
A tune in those pages, still played on stages
got christened my friends, that day, guaranteed.

mayor harrison's fedora – reel

Once again the title just begs to be explored. A great tune no
doubt and the poem accurately reflects the origin of the title.
Honest!

16 - the twelve pins
(Original title by Charlie Lennon)

The tallest man you ever saw,
(that is, the distance from his jaw
to heel almost stretched eight feet)
said in a manner brisk and neat
'Sir, I'm in the market for a suit.'

He stooped and hunched going in
(a hitch for one so tall and thin),
the tailor said, 'Sir, please be seated.
You'll be amazed when it's completed.
Kindly now remove your left boot."

Upon the chair the man reclined
needle and thread were thus entwined,
"His arms will both require a yard."
He read from his little fabric card
listing all the patterns to be found.

He thought upon his magic pins
that would be needed on the shins
and sleeves never mind the back.
The tiny twelve from their rack
spread like silver spears on the ground.

He cut and measured with tape afire,
his Irish tweed, the world's desire,
till the makings slowly came to life.
Round the buttons with a knife
he sliced as if cutting wheaten bread.

Pins one to four this expert placed
he said, "No bigger task I have faced.
Sir you'll be the toast of Dublin town."
Pins five to nine stout held down
the inside cloth alive in black and red.

Pin ten he used around the collar.
"They'll consider you no doubt a scholar
when along the Temple Bar you stroll."
He then quickly fetched another roll,
pin eleven held all round the waist.

"Pin twelve until this day has lain
unused but I shall avoid disdain".
and stick it in the pocket at your breast.
In a flash of light around his chest
the suit appeared exactly to his taste.

"This spell or charm that you command
is the greatest seen in old Ireland,"
said the fellow high and long of stride.
"Thank you sir but if you confide
with any the stitches all will come apart.

"Oh, ok" replied the lengthened chap
"I shall dodge with silence that mishap.
My new adventure here and now begins.
The tailor replaced his twelve bright pins
wondering when next a suit he'd start.

the twelve pins - Reel

Des Leech (RIP) from Dublin was a tailor as well as a brilliant traditional musician and singer. His son Stephen is one of our oldest, tallest friends. I dedicate the poem to them.

17 - when sick is it tea you want?
(Trad title)

"When sick is it tea you want?"
"It is when you're feeling blue.
What type of tea do you have?"
"I have tea! Will that not do!?"

"Ah surely, that would be great
but my days of Tetley are gone.
I saw this one in the Spar
I think it was called Ceylon?

Chamomile would do the trick
or Oolong or herbal or green?"
"Uh huh, that sounds very grand."
'neath taps the kettle was leaned.

"I've Punjana, Lyon's and Barry's,
(as Irish as Irish can be!)
I wouldn't dampen the others,
a waste of hot water for me.

How do you dunk a digestive
into a mug of Earl Grey?
Thon stuff would ruin a wake,
don't care what anyone says!

My aunt would spin in her grave,
what future could she foresee
if someone came in with a cup
and it full of strawberry tea?"

"You know you may have a point
but teas are as varied as wine.
Next time you ask, 'Are you sick?'
I think I'll just say, "I'm fine!""

when sick is it tea you want? - jig

My great auntie Maggie read tealeaves. I was thinking of her when writing this one. Tea has definitely spread its wings.

18 - the floating crowbar
(Original title by Brendan McGlinchey)

On noticing yonder a gull
chewing hard on a chip,
the crow above circled down
and with a curling lip
said, "My curious cousin
really I am rather sad.
I've never been out to sea,
there's so much fun to be had."

The gulping gull swallowed hard
and a little in shock
almost choked as the crow
feelings to him did unlock.
"Oh how we long to float
bobbing atop the waves
but this desire for my kind
we must take to our graves."

"Well that's a lot of boloney!"
the gull did loudly reply,
as quickly gathered all round
a flock of them up in the sky.
My friends and I have decreed
every crow from right now
will enjoy a watery gift,
just let me show you how."

The crow let forth a croak
and followed out to the ledge
the white web-toed collection
landing right on the edge.
From there he easy surveyed
with lights, fireworks and all
signs saying, 'Free drink all day.'
and 'only black suits for the ball.'

"Yes, we built it last night
for you and all of your kin.
A floating crow bar if you will
and only you crows get in."
In Rostrevor near to the shore,
eight flaps as the crow flies
you'll hear them this very day
cawing, "One more for the skies!"

the floating crowbar - reel

I just learned recently that Brendan McGlinchey wrote this classic tune also. I had wrongly assumed it was 'trad'. You just never know. I wonder if I wore a black cloak could I get in?

41

19 - cornelius curtin's big balloon
(Trad title)

What a glorious craft, all ready to go
blasted with flame and her canopy high.
Into the basket we sailed for the sky
quickly departing the excited below.

Cornelius himself, dapperly dressed,
top hat and britches, shoes a-gleaming.
Higher and higher I felt I was dreaming
and with views was completely impressed.

Sure we soared over hill, valley and glen
over the villages and many small towns
till our pilot's brow deepening frowns
"We're going down, I fear, just can't say when.

Do you see that falcon headed due south?
I'm afraid his talons have caused quite a rip
and will considerably shorten our trip."
I scarce believed what came from his mouth.

"Shorten?" says I, in the midst of a sweat
"We're now over water, with land far behind."
Slowly I felt I was losing my mind
"Hmm this might be the most dangerous yet."

"Yet!" I replied now my dread was complete.
"I've my whole life ahead, it cannot end here!"
He pulled on a rope in an effort to steer.
It came down and lay in a ball at his feet.

"Oh that's not good," he said looking shocked.
"Perhaps with the fabric we could make sails?"
Not far below I spied dolphins and whales
and sharks beyond had jaws all unlocked.

"Damn you Cornelius!" Aloud I did bawl.
We tipped into water all splashes and drips.
The last words I heard to come from his lips
were, "This indeed... is curtains for us all."

cornelius curtin's big balloon – jig

I couldn't believe this was a real tune, it sounds like a movie. Again, a poet's delight. (You may see this tune also called Cornelius Curtin's Hot Air Balloon).

20 - the three sea captains
(Trad title)

"When all at sea, you see, your man, him and me,
there's one thing that will straighten up the bow.
Be it gale or swirling tide or zephyrs on a spree
smooth sailing's secret I'll tell you now.

Grab your instrument of choice little does it mean
if the fiddle is your favourite or accordion or flute.
The choice of key is key to prevent you turning green
and stop certain solids from flying out the chute.

Beneath the churning froth and the angry hurricane,
atop the whirlpool circling and the jagged stony shore,
deafened by the thunder and flooded by the rain
the key in which you play will cease chaos evermore.

Cedric, Cyril and myself, (to me Cecil was bequeathed),
have sailed Ireland round from to toe to head
and when we feared that our last breath was breathed,
panic? Not at all, we got our instruments instead.

We have nothing against F, no quarrelling with A
G can bring joy at times of that there is no doubt.
E in equal measure has its charms most would say
and all related minors certainly will out.

High atop the ocean blue, dancing round the reef
the three of us while on that raging main
with jigs, slides or polkas it is our belief
the key of C will guide us when the tune turns again."

the three sea captains - jig

We live beside the sea these days and this one found me quite quickly. In terms of C tunes though sometimes they find me too quickly! This, of course, is in G.

2) - kitty got a clinking coming from the fair
(Trad title)

In Ballycastle by the sea
every August on a spree
so many folk there will be
you'll not believe it true.
The Lammas Fair so well known
for salty dulce (nearby grown)
and yellowman has jaws a-goin'
you should see them chew!

First of all you'd see her hair
blowing like confetti there
a bush of blonde in the air
her laughing all the while.
A pint of cider in each hand
her fiddle waiting on the stand
things never went as planned
such was her vacant style.

Into polkas, jigs and reels,
the entire tavern on its heels
hups, shouts, stomps, squeals
with fun the place was fed.
But poor oul Kitty at the door
says, "We'll just have one more,"
as in another bunch did pour
the door hit her on the head.

She was dazed and dizzy too
"Who clinked me? Was it you?"
Her poor oul eye black n blue
and her nose in awful shape.
But steadied soon up she stood
and staggering as best she could
her mouth was a sea of blood
she sat down in a hape.

She grabbed her pint, next her bow
Took a swig, then reels did flow.
God she gave a deadly show
the Lammas had not seen.
She gave her face a hearty rub,
the heartbeat of the session hub
what a night in wee Tom's pub
the best there's ever been.

kitty got a clinking coming from the fair – reel

The Lammas Fair in Ballycastle is a wondrous experience. As if from nowhere her small streets fill to the hilt with all manner of stall, seller and customer. It's a great celebration of hustle and bustle. The Kitty in question knows it well!

22 - the mouse in the toaster
(Original title by Brendan Mulholland)

As if giving birth without anaesthetic
or like an oul drunk and him paralytic
akin to seeing a ghost in the attic
came a frightening scream from below.
Says I to myself, "She's stood on a nail.
Or some damn thief has half-inched my ale."
Whatever the cause of this merciless wail
my face I'd better fast show.

In y-fronts and vest I ventured at speed,
she gave me a look meaning 'better take heed!'
"Christ," she roared. "I'm in undoubted need
of three double rums and a gin!"
The smell of singe raced up my nose.
"What the hell's burning do you suppose?"
Says she, "It's a mouse! In its death throes.
For bread crumbs his end did begin."

I saw silver then smoke quick emanating
and there in the toaster as if hibernating
his teeth, tongue and jaws once salivating
and the rest of him crisp as a twig.
"Mickey," says I, "sure you near got away
but deep in the garden you I will lay."
The toaster all clean I grabbed me some tay,
as deals go it wasn't that big.

But her curse words flowed like lava and oil
"Bring that in here your head I will boil.
There'll be you and the rodent under the soil
Have I made that perfectly clear?"
"Crystal," says I then trudged to the store.
The one with air fryers and dryers and more.
"Mouse proof toasters?" "Aye at the door.
first one ever sold in here!"

the mouse in the toaster - Reel

Brendan Mulholland from Glenavy has been playing the flute since the days of black and white TV! He is now a much sought after performer and tutor. His tune and this piece were inspired by the true tale he shared a while ago. (I'm not sure Aisling is over it yet!)

23 - soap on the bristles
(Original title by Catherine Uí Sheanáin)

It often seemed
a peculiar place to sit,
to me at least, (until I learned
the workings of the house).
The wooden base sandwiched
between course hairs,

short and shorter sat up
proud in the kitchen,
near the sink. Alongside it
the pimpled plastic
pad meant to curtail
the varied wanderings of soap
helped create a rather
understated double act.

The smell of a cooked dinner
sets the scene, potatoes
in their half off jackets
steaming on a platter, gravy
bubbling like dark lava
on the stove. The whoosh

of a fan designed to keep
the windows from dripping.
The door opens as near
to five o'clock as makes
no difference. The little shock
of blonde shouts
'granda' but is momentarily
denied. He has one more

duty to seal the day. He grabs
up the little punk brush,
hands covered in oil and years.
They swamp the soap until
a lather emanates
and is rubbed in deep.

He scrapes under his nails,
tiny hands tug his overalls
impatient and excited.
The water falls in mixed colours
gradually clearing until ready.
He turns in generations
and lifts his grand-daughter
up almost to the clouds.

soap on the bristles – reel

Soap on the Bristles

for my Dad (RIP)
Dec 21 Catherine Uí S.

This is a beautiful tune written by my wife Catherine for her dad Padraig McLean (RIP). It was my honour to know him and witness regularly the scenes depicted in the lines opposite. He was a gentleman and much loved by all who knew him. The little girl in the poem is our daughter, Katie.

24 - the pigeon on the gate
(Trad title)

The pigeon sat upon the gate and shed a single tear
"I'm afraid for me it is too late, I can't fly from here."
A cuckoo and a field mouse heard her tearful plea
And both were curious to know the reason for this scene

The pigeon wiped away a tear and said, "This is my tale."
She began to speak in mortal fear as they were joined by
a snail
"The hawk knows I'm grounded and he'll be calling soon
And I'll be another victim before the clouds reveal the
moon."

The cuckoo interrupted then, saying, "I can't see what's
wrong
I'm flying since I don't know when, have a go it won't take
long."
"But there's the whole trouble," sadly the pigeon said
"Its my right wing and my left wing they're going to see me
dead."

"Explain," said the field mouse, "what on earth do you
mean?
You should be in a madhouse what you say is obscene!
Just flap your wings together, for you a simple task."
"Ahh!" sighed the pigeon, "it's the impossible you ask."

"You see my wings have fallen out, they won't speak at all
The right wing wants to scream and shout the left wing
won't play ball
It thinks I should fly less and maybe get more pay
And I'm stuck in the middle and really have no say."

The snail then popped out an eye and said, "Don't you
see?
Someone like me could never fly; two flaps and you'd be
free
I hate to quote the obvious but dusk is right on time
And the hawk is now approaching, on you he's set to
dine."

The pigeon gave each wing a glance and said, "Now listen here,
The really is my last chance, from trouble help me steer."
But too long set in their feud neither deemed to start
And the hawk swooped down to the gate and pierced the pigeon's heart

From the safety of the clover the cuckoo and the snail
Knew her life was over and both began to pale
The field mouse counted his blessings and went into his hide
And all three knew no good can come when each hates the other side.

the pigeon on the gate – Reel

Sometimes a poem waits to be discovered. This piece ventured out into the world a while ago as a song only to decide it wasn't quite ready. Happily, after some gentle encouragement, it's ready now.

25 - the last house in connaught
(Trad title aka Dinny O'Brien's)

If you're looking for stones we've plenty of them
or rushes and gorse in those we are rich.
The trees we know from soil to the stem,
we have names for cattle and every ditch.

But come here to me know I'll tell you a tale
of a man and his fiddle the finest yet made.
Dinny O'Brien supped long on the dark ale
and the world would whisht whenever he played.

The house he constructed sat close to the cliff
that stretched to the sea and wildness below.
The roof it was thatched with beams long and stiff
withstanding whatever gales there did blow.

So came a Saturday, the first past the moon
when neighbours would call laden with wares
and as if by decree Tom started the tunes
and came quick after the jigs and slow airs.

Marie sang her ballad as was the tradition
Stephen then called them all for to hush.
Catherine herself gave a dazzling rendition
of a wondrous reel called the Leitrim Thrush.

For as long as waves have on beaches rolled
the ceilidhs at Dinny's deep filled the night.
Till that murky evening, sad truth be told,
some hallion introduced the electric light.

None in the company could ever have foreseen
the change that occurred at the flick of a switch.
Though useful of course that which had been
was lost to places darkness only can stitch.

The last house in Connaught thus was attached
to the grid and a different world had arrived
My memory sings of those evenings unmatched
where half truths and old stories thrived.

the last house in connaught – Reel

I heard once that the great guitarist Arty McGlynn had
bemoaned the invention of central heating. His logic was that
with heat all around the house there was no hub i.e. the fireside
and so a scattering of sorts took place in the family. Hard to
argue with him. This informed my thinking when writing this
piece.

26 - the maid behind the bar
(Trad title)

Her green eyes sparkle like the glasses
elegantly there she passes
through lines standing two and three.
Her gleaming smile warms the hearts
of the crowd as she starts
to pull, pour and set the nectar free.

Her hair so long in cascades brown
on her shoulders falling round
like water flowing in a morning stream.
Her necklace more attention brings,
in each ear two golden rings,
I wonder if in truth she is a dream.

So somewhere next to hope I stand
and wonder if upon her hand
some day I may place a diamond bright.
She floats above the loud furore
thirst can at times implore,
a beacon on an often stormy night.

Should fate provide the circumstance
I shall my feelings then advance
hidden all these years as they are.
She is called away and I depart
trusting I may yet win the heart
of the gentle maid behind the bar.

the maid behind the bar - reel

My mum Barbara and her sister, Isobel, ran The Cove Bar
outside Newry for many years. It was a great bar with great
memories. I learned much of life from working there and highly
recommend it as a career. I dedicate this piece to my mum for
all the love, advice, patience and of course...pints!

27 - mary's midnight garden
(Original title by Catherine Uí Sheanáin)

About it flutter different wings
perhaps a child might see.
As they land on different things
I wish that child was me.
All at once their magic brings
such true tranquillity.
On every leaf surely clings
much sweet serenity.

They are of an Ireland old
before the days of man.
Summer sun and winter cold
helped draw up the plan
to visit here in times untold
they will do while they can.
Nature's beauties they behold
and millennia they span.

In the dead of night I went
my heart did beat aloud
I wondered if tonight's event
in mystery would shroud
As the chimes all were spent
the flowers soon had bowed
As magic to my eyes was lent
I never felt so proud

The fairies of the glen appeared
each with a flash of light
Nothing there at all I feared
that cool and secret night
How they danced and loudly cheered
around that sacred site.
Her midnight garden so revered
forever burning bright

mary's midnight garden - reel

Marys Midnight Garden.

For my mum (Rip)
Dec 21 Catherine Uis.

Another beautiful and joyous tune written by Catherine for her mum, Mary McLean (RIP). If ever there was someone who loved the outdoors and gardening in particular it was her. She is sorely missed but we play this tune in her honour as often as we can.

28 - The Piper's Daughter
(Trad title)

Her name alas I cannot say
just happy I that heard her play
down at the river every day
her music ebbed and flowed.
Beside the stone beneath the tree
the river sang her melody
and happy in their company
the world about me slowed.

In merry hops her fingers danced
birds and insects all entranced
the air around sound enhanced
I breathed it there deep down
With her notes she decorated
the fields and hedges celebrated
sorrows swiftly were negated
and eased away my frown

A snapping twig my hide revealed
she turned to where I had kneeled,
I quickly to her there appealed
'from whom this did you learn?'
Surprised but smiling she replied
in my eyes my mother spied
a piper's heart and so relied
that these skills I would earn.'

'She taught the lesson old and true
practice knows what it must do
and since then I've paid what's due
to share with all each tune.'
'If I may your tale I'll spread
and in the glen it shall be read
in books so that those ahead
will know her playing soon.'

the piper's daughter - jig

You don't have to be mad to learn the pipes but...My sister in law Marie and her daughter Aoife both play pipes as does our son Tóla. The generational quality of passing down tradition from one generation to the next guided me here.

29 - an Fáinne Óir (the gold Ring)
(Trad title)

"If to be my husband, you must catch the sun.
Once it sits upon my hand our marriage is begun."

"It will be my honour to deliver you your prize.
Keep your eyes upon the shore, your heart upon the skies."

To the east he sped away and on his lips a tune,
"I will marry you my love," he sang beneath the moon.

To the kingdom's highest peak he rode in fierce pursuit
and waited for the sun to rise his mood so resolute.

All he had to do he thought was simply see the dawn
and in his shield collect the sun as brightly then it shone.

The dark of night yielded to that glorious fiery ball
grinning wide he yelled aloud, "this shan't be hard at all."

But he slowly learned of course that it was far beyond,
no silver shield ever forged the sun could carry on.

It blazed its way into the sky but darken did his heart
as slowly from the mountain top in defeat he did depart.

He turned again to see the foe that caused his tears to fall
and noticed then his armour gleam, "There's hope after all.

Perhaps if not the sun itself I'll capture here its fire
and from this golden plated suit she'll see my heart's
desire."

At the forge the smith awoke hearing, "Stoke your
flames.
This golden armour melt it down till just a band
remains."

The heat by the bellows fanned matched the molten
gold
and piece by piece the armour fell till a ring he did
behold.

Captured in its circled form the brightness of the star
and to her window quick he rode in night's darkest
hour.

The court arose and greeted him, she in front did stand
"I trust you have the very sun to place upon my hand?"

"The task you set no man could do but listen if you will
My head sighed impossible but my heart drove me still.

I offer you the dawn itself and how my heart would sing
if you agree to wear upon your hand this golden ring."

"Our love will burn ever bright," she said on raising
high,
"this ring our bond as there is twixt the sun, earth and
sky."

an Fáinne Óir (the Gold Ring) – Reel

A grand adventure for a grand tune. One often wonders at
times where the tunes come from. This one has a starter,
main course and dessert. A favourite in sessions throughout
the country.

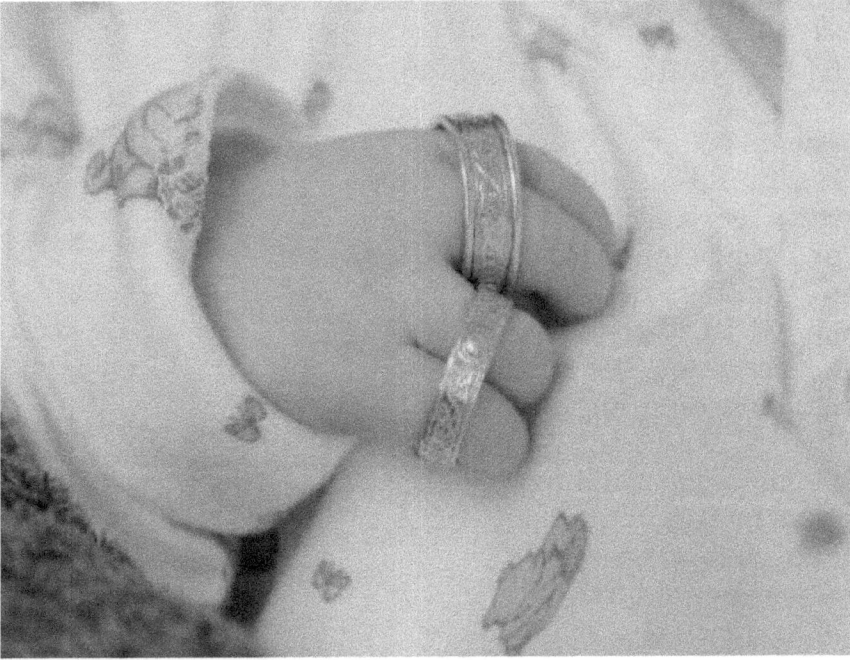

These gold rings were placed on our children, Katie and Tolá's hands not long after their arrival way back in 2002 and 2009. I don't think they'd fit them now!

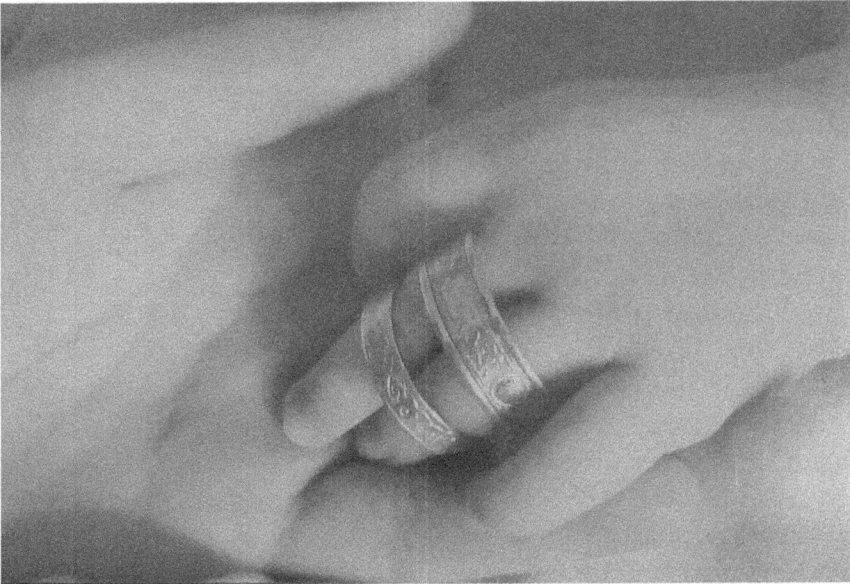

30 - the cat's meow
(Original title Joanie Madden)

The end approaches.
Her breathing raises
the sheet a little
and we watch, waiting.
In moments of levity
an old story praises
her fortitude. We smile,
laughter creating

memories of childhood
days in Toor.
Patrick long wonders
where her old friend
has gone. The cool
black whose purr
spoke of contentment
and the lend

of heat on her lap.
"Haven't seen her,"
says Marie. "Maybe
she knows a bit more
than us." Silence
reclaims the room, sure
of its import. Catherine
opens the door

to sleep and prepare.
The sitters leave
and hope against hope.
Patrick dozes
until at the window,
in time to grieve
it appears, calling
to her, and discloses

her passing. The
mood moves again.
Hearing of the return
we wonder how
it knew. The mystery
is an old refrain,
found in the music
of the cat's meow.

the cat's meow – jig

My late mother in law, Mary McLean, was a beautiful, kind and gentle woman. She adored her children and grandchildren. Sadly she passed away a few years ago and we miss her to this day. This poem touches on true events on the night of her passing.

31 - The Sailor on the Rock
(Trad title)

Fingers like the ropes themselves,
coarse, long and rough,
his hands fan out like bellows
stoking up the flame.
His arms speak of strength and toil,
rules of the game
that brings him out to sea again
beyond the craggy bluff.

Atop his head a scarf in red
soaking up the sweat
that if escapes drowns his brow
as distance is surveyed.
In his ears two hoops of gold
good luck to him conveyed
a Spanish fleet's watery grave
gave the finest treasures yet.

In Ballintoy his vessel waits
patiently restrained
till over foam and swirling tide
it scalpels through the waves.
Beyond the cliffs of Rathlin
and the secrets of her caves
he'll venture on to Islay
and the bar all whiskey stained.

The spray against his skin
sea-scorched freely rolls
in droplets to the deck
and on the steering wheel.
The salmon to his swaying nets
he entices with a reel,
played aloud his whistle is
in honour of lost souls.

His sturdy ship is prepared
he christened her 'The Rock',
the dolphin pods know her keel
and often race beside.
Into dreams this sailor goes
with moonlight to confide,
the riddles of the Straits of Moyle
he determines to unlock.

the sailor on the Rock– Reel

We know a few sailors and boatmen who traverse regularly the sea of Moyle to Rathlin Island and beyond. To have an understanding of the sea is power indeed.

32 - mulligan's ice cream
(Original title by John Mackel)

The back of my throat was like the Sahara,
gritty and dry with no moisture at all.
"This may be the end," I thought in a terror
a hangover this bad I could not recall.

The craic it was mighty in old Ennis town,
the want of Guinness was easily met.
One after the other they swiftly went down,
the sessions we played, the finest played yet.

But in the day light my eyes readjusted
from the warm, easy glow of the tavern before.
Two squinting lines, the oul' brain had rusted
with all of the liquid I did happily pour.

My comrades about like soldiers were maimed
with whisky and wine and cider as well.
A morgue wouldn't take them, poitín was blamed
for John's disappearance where none could tell.

Into the car in our pity well wrapped,
we heaved in our bodies like bags of cement.
Some sat in shock while some of us napped
the snoring was brutal, my ears it did dent.

After a crossroads quipped the boul' Mark,
"Lads it is time our fortunes to turn."
The words 'ice' and 'cream' sung out like a lark,
relief at last as indigestion did burn.

There was raspberry ripple, chocolate too.
There was strawberry, lemon and lime.
There were pokes and sliders and all I could do
was shout, "God, we're here just in time!"

We licked and slurped like colts at the trough
the taste buds had seen resurrection.
I crunched at the end and each morsel scoffed,
for the cure this place was perfection!

mulligan's ice cream - reel

*Delighted to display another original tune here from the prolific
writer and fiddle player John Mackel. Along with 'The Glenavy
Gang' John has been keeping traditional music alive near Lough
Neagh's shore for many years.*

33 - O'carolan's concerto
(Original title by Turlough O'Carolan)

Ironic that it should begin with such light,
(darkness for so long his companion).

He detonates notes on stretched strings
and resonating in a curved wooden canyon

they demand the ear not be inattentive.
The higher octaves splash into consideration

whilst those on the basses slide crocodile like
into water, with subtle, skilful moderation.

His fingers grip and release with such alacrity
one might almost consider them to be sewing

together a garment made only of musical air.
Who might wear it but the person knowing

the melody is gift or Planxty from the player.
Beneath the high ceiling of wood and stone

they sit frozen and warm, still and yet moved
by the riches woven from skin unto bone.

The moments that follow shall replace echoes
with a proliferation of whispers and wine.

The kitchen calls and I am bound to carry
plates wondering how this sound to define.

o'carolan's concerto - reel

The blind piper and composer Turlough O'Carolan holds a very special place in the tradition. His music echoes the classical pieces of Europe at the time and have each established themselves in many players' repertoires. I imagined here a serving girl listening to a recital from O'Carolan himself.

34 - the king of the fairies
(Trad title)

The mist about the fairy thorn had too long been in place
and in every waking moment his halls the king did pace.
'Without that tune I'm finished, I surely cannot face
the witch at Hanging River and that is my disgrace.'

'She means to take what's ours, she means to rule us all.
Her cruelty and hatred would have us each one fall
upon our knees and beg to heed her beck and call.
And now without our music victory's hopes are small.'

'Oh king, my king,' came a voice, young, strong and
brave.
'I know a place in which I'll find the tune us all to save.
'Where oh where?' replied the king, his hands high did
wave.
'It's in my harp,' she answered. 'She'll not us enslave.'

'What wondrous news this is but please tell me true,
where be found the saving notes and just who are you?'
'I am Katie of the Tree where the mighty buzzards flew
when battling the crows and banished them from view.'

'You know the tune of which I speak? Hard his question
fell.
'I do indeed. I'll play it now so your army you can tell.'
She plucked the strings in order and all our hearts did
swell
When a loud 'hurrah' from the king echoed like a bell.

The Hanging River found them all just as the sun
appeared
and soon the cailleach captured was oh how loud we
cheered.
'From now on your wickedness from memory will be
cleared
and in their stead let this tune around us all be steered.'

74

the king of the fairies - hornpipe

'Na daoine maithe' or 'na síoga' are just two of the names in Irish for fairies. All Irish people have an innate respect for the fairies who always reside never too far away.

ᚷ - queen of the fair
(Trad title)

The harvest safely gathered
in the darkened store
lies safe to help us face
the winter chill.
The fingers tying sheaves
need to toil no more
our stocks would have to do
for good or ill.

Exiled years meant a loss
of revelry and cause
bound as one in pain
we rallied round.
Till there upon the sea
our sorrows all did pause,
we see ashore her vessel
touch the ground.

We celebrate the season
with our loaves and mass
(Lughnasagh or Lammas,
both are known)
And back at last from Rathlin,
on seas just like glass
from young princess to woman
she has grown.

The excitement of the traders
setting up their wares
the people running eager
to the sands.
The salted seaweed smiles
and sweetened yellow stares
of kids eager to get
some in their hands.

76

Returned again amongst her own
her beauty ever bright
the old concerns have
lifted from the air
Taisie of the glen
how you shine this August night
christened forever now,
Queen of the fair.

35 - queen of the fair - jig

In myth and legend Princess Taisie was daughter of King Dorm of Rathlin Island. She had many suitors and battles were fought for the right to be her husband. I imagine here however the view of the common people and how proud they are to see her become a woman queen. Again the fair I have in mind is the Lammas Fair, you'll really have to go!

36 - toss the feathers
(Trad title)

For the fifteenth time the night before
they rehearsed beside the kitchen door.

A deed that would in legend stay
if with it they could get away.

The object of their daring raid
had that day ten fried eggs laid

On Sunday past she laid three poached,
no wonder then they soon approached.

They knew as well she laid five boiled
and ever since the two had toiled

scheming to get that hen alone
and feast on omelette's from then one

"I've no doubt she lays them scrambled,"
said Pete as the wood they rambled

"Yip," said Bob in his overalls
"Who cares about cholesterol?"

As the light from evening faded
excitement on their minds invaded.

To have that hen that lays 'em cooked
meant no detail overlooked.

Security round the barn was tight
with chicken wire, all sorts of light

but Pete had cutters sharp and true
Bob burst bulbs with his point two-two.

Round her head Pete threw the bag
he used to feed his aging nag.

Bob as quickly grabbed her feet
the heist was soon half complete.

78

The other half was getting out
in mortal fear the two did shout.

as suddenly rolled a mighty stone
just like In-diana Jones!

Poor Bob held the hen in close,
"Toss it quick!" said Pete, "Ye dose!"

Bob threw and the fence he cleared
but 'neath the rock he disappeared.

Into the night ran Pete high-tailed
a gang of bloodhounds on his trail.

Last I heard he had on six stone,
munching on his eggs alone.

He sighs and shakes some Cayenne
"The best laid plans of mice...a hen."

toss the feathers - reel

*Unusually this title covers two different tunes which requires
clarification should you be asked to play it. I prefer the above
setting although the other is a fine tune too.*

37 - the maid at the spinning wheel
(Trad title aka The Hag at the Spinning Wheel)

Her beauty is eternal
shining 'neath the sun,
of all the faces ever seen
they say hers is the one
to drive the men astray.
Her hair like diving swallows
arriving with the eve
rolls about her shoulders
to make a man believe
magic comes his way.

Sitting next her wooden wheel
reeling in her dreams,
furling onto bobbins
slowly showing streams
and rivers of the heart.
If generous be your soul
and your intentions dear
a meeting maybe lies ahead
on a pathway clear
romance there to start.

But if your mind is errant
and twisted like a brier
no lady fair will you see
with yarns to acquire
but a hag there a-weaving.
You ensnared like the wool
about her all would be
captured in your thoughts
never to be free
in darkness there a-grieving.

Be mindful of your wishes
when you fix your eye
on any maiden spinning
or simply walking by,
fate is on the line.
Be courteous and charming
and your dealings fair
the eye of the beholder
is the maiden in the chair
in wisdom all entwined.

the maid at the spinning wheel - jig

I read somewhere that this tune had two names, The Maid at the Spinning Wheel or The Hag at the Spinning Wheel. This duality inspired the lines in the poem.

38 - the contradiction
(Trad title)

"I think we should have blue, a calming colour no doubt."
"No, not blue it's awful what are you talking about?"

"Surely you wouldn't pick green? The coldest colour of all."
"Green is the colour of nature dear, rivers and trees so tall."

"Goodness knows but not me. Perhaps we could go red?"
"Now you're just having a laugh. Are you away in the head?

Sure how we he ever sleep? He'd think his wee room was on fire!"
"Honest to God woman dear, frustration you do inspire!"

"What are we eating tonight? I really fancy Chinese."
"After my stomach last week I'll have spuds if you please."

A wee bit of butter and salt, your father he would be proud."
"He'd think, 'get what you want' and he would think it out loud!"

"Spain is great for a break. Do you think that we could go there?"
"It's full of people gone mad! You can't beat Larne for fresh air."

"Does my bum look big in this dress? Can't find a thing to put on.
We should go shopping tomorrow, where has my waistline gone?"

"No room left my dear. Your wardrobe's the size of a trailer.
I've had this suit since the eighties." "Indeed, you're no friend to the tailor!"

"Put on something romantic. When did you last buy flowers?"
"Seriously love, come on, those films drag on for hours.

He falls in love with her and then she does nothing but cry.
Then he'll ride in on his horse and neither yours eyes will be dry."

"Sure you shout like mad at the football, those ejits rolling about.
Give them a hurl in Croke Park, that's where the real men run out."

"You're never wrong," he answers. "You're always right," says she.
"Maybe at last we've found something on which we both can agree!"

the contradiction – Reel

I love this tune. No I don't!

39 - the lost boy
(Original title by Johnny Murphy)

Stolen; removed from nurture.
Tall shadows add the torture
of loss to who and what I am.
High ceilings are decades away.
Full classrooms oft hear me pray
and confess, sing loud a psalm

as if I should be grateful for fear.
So goes my youth captured here
seeking the comforts of love.
Their old suit scrapes on my skin;
a cheap gift. They send me out in
to the world with a shove.

At seventeen I stand up reborn
unearthing new strength, shorn
of cruelty and empty years.
I now hear my voice in the throngs
of Clonmel, whose sweet songs
calm the worst of my fears.

I see my own country break free
in part and live one day to see
liberty for us all realised.
Oh Ireland please hear your son
loudly I pray that when it is done
gone are those most despised.

In my family and faith I survive;
in my children, may they all thrive.
In happiness let each be crowned.
That my journey comes to its end
I will rest well and proudly contend
that thanks to him, I am found.

the lost boy – air

I was honoured to learn the intensely personal story behind this beautiful slow air. It represents triumph over adversity in a darker Ireland. I thank our good friend, fiddle player and maker Johnny Murphy from Ballymena for sharing it with me. In honour of John Murphy (RIP)

40 - ᴅʀᴏᴡsʏ mᴀᴄᴄɪᴇ
(Trad title)

"Margaret my dear are you tired?
Your eyes are bloodshot I see.
Perhaps you're ill? Fate has conspired
to reduce your joie de vivre?"

"Each morning you come in for to start
your stride is slow and fatigued.
A reason maybe you'd care to impart?
Honestly, I'm quite intrigued?"

"I surmised that you were with child.
A cause for no doubt for malaise.
Has a rogue you wrongly beguiled,
filling your head full of praise?"

"Young ladies are delicate and true,
not designed for rigour or toil.
Have we not done what's best for you?
Really your future you'll spoil!"

"Oh, you arrogant oaf of a man.
I labour because I must do.
Your pay is hardly warm in my hand
before debts have it all removed."

"But this day take heed is my last.
I have been singing each night.
Proudly I say that I have amassed
enough to make my future bright."

"The girls in my shift think the same,
together for Dublin we're bound.
We can see now we're not to blame
for your business crashing to ground."

"So farewell to you Mister Gray,
I shall be drowsy no more.
Nor will my sisters who from today
shall bloom like never before."

Drowsy maggie - Reel

Another of the tunes trad players grow up learning. I often wondered who Maggie was and why she was so tired. I like the idea of a gentle revolution and fulfilling one's potential once the shackles are broken.

41 - ᴅusᴄy winᴅowsills
(Trad title)

There upon the windowsill as the room she cleaned
shapes that made her stop whereon she stood.
"Oh my," she gasped then on the wall she leaned,
what she saw were foot prints in the wood!

"Youngsters maybe playing with their Christmas toys,"
she went to get some answers from the two
But as she left the room began a pleasant noise;
music, songs... a wondrous hullaballoo.

Next the children at her waist appeared on either side
and whispered, "Mum, we've heard this before."
The three of them at once wondered should they hide
but slowly stuck their heads round the door

There upon the windowsill a ceilidh in full swing!
A fairy playing tunes with a fiddle and a bow.
Some of them were dancing, some were on the wing
What was going on they really didn't know

There were tiny pints of Guinness, tables everywhere,
accordions and a flute all playing tunes.
There were bodhráns and banjos, hands in the air
And who'd believe a fairy on the spoons!

"No wonder it's so dusty," mum said with a moan
then saw her children halfway cross the room
"Get back here," she whispered, feeling quite alone
As a fairy started dancing with a broom

Three big faces staring down mother said, "Bíciúin!"
and forty faces stared right back as one.
"My friends and I implore our ceilidh please don't ruin
We'll tidy up the window when we're done!"

The children said, "Oh please!" Mummy said, "OK...
A tidy house is all I want to see."
"Deal," said the fairies and at every break of day
says Mum, "No dusty windowsills for me!"

ᴅᴜꜱᴛʏ ᴡɪɴᴅᴏᴡꜱɪʟʟꜱ - ᴊɪɢ

What better reason to have dust on the windowsills than a fairy ceilidh! Growing up fairies played a big part in our imagination. As well as being magical and mischievous they help us view nature in a unique and beautiful way and treat it with respect.

42 - jackson's morning brush
(Trad title)

The early winds breezed by like a swallow
a contrast to the tempests not long before.
A night spent releasing tunes into heads
and hearts; all needed feet to implore.

Rarely was a kitchen so big and so small
as inside they crammed, together and tight.
Laces on laces, old boots hard on heels
and careful steps set all through the night.

Concerns played on as loud in his head,
there was something amiss with higher ranges.
No matter his press the bag could not force
the reed to sing required octave changes.

He thought on the dust raised up off the floor
as they hopped and leapt in tumults of tunes
'Perhaps it settled in the throat of the chanter?
If that's the case I had better mend soon.'

He sat near the orchard, exploding in green
and saw in dismay the invasion contained.
'What might I use to restore all her glories?'
Four buzzard's feathers hope now maintained.

He fastened them close, bound like an arrow
and forced all deep down quickly to twist.
Out came pollution and his new resolution
'The morning brush means no note is missed.'

42 - Jackson's morning brush - jig

Sometimes a tune title is baffling. What brush could this be referring to? With a little research I found that pipers would clean out their pipes to maintain the best possible sound. This piece is a look at how that tradition was done for the very first time...allegedly.

43 - The Jolly Tinker
(Trad title)

The rims were thin on his wheels, causing
an uneasy side to side. Not too concerning
from the driver's bench but frequent nausea
had overcome his black cat in the turning.

Cantankerousness had recently shaped
his old pony's mood. He knew well the shoes
were down to the nail. They'd been scraped
away over miles. It was time he paid his dues

to McCabe the blacksmith of Donegal town.
'You in there ye blaggard?' he called aloud
Striding from the dark door and setting down
his hammer McCabe grinned widely and bowed,

"The Jolly Tinker," he offered in greeting.
"The Merry Blacksmith I would dare presume?"
Indeed. I did not think we would be meeting
today when on my hot anvil I did resume.

Might I guess it's the rims that need repairing?"
"And shoes for herself, she's thin on the ground."
"And payment this time? Perhaps you'll be airing
that song on the banjo in Newry you found."

"I've something brand new, a tune in my head
that appeared like the sun as soundly I slept
Instead of a song I shall play that instead
and your name in history will forever be kept."

The wheels better trundled when all completed,
the pony's new fittings returned all his light.
The tinker and blacksmith in music competed
playing tunes for each other all through the night.

The Jolly Tinker - Reel

Another reference to a member of the travelling community. It wasn't that long ago the 'tinkerman' had an almost wizard like quality to him and his visits were an event in any town. Sadly, these days their treatment leaves much to be desired.

44 - The Drunken Landlady
(Trad title)

It was a rarity for her to be all askew,
normally she hold sway among the settled.
Tonight though she was home away from home,
back in Tipperary, its paths bloom petalled.

Gone from her shoulders the unending weight
of loss too young. Instead, her favourite song
sung with arms aloft at the dividing door
somewhere in the valley near Sliabh na mBan.

We looked up from our small stools at a table
adorned with black gold, instruments followed
her words. From the wee room suddenly a host
of chorus voices and as one the bar swallowed

happy to join her on this infrequent journey.
The mixer in her whiskey looked on proudly.
Together they had sated a thousand thirsts
'You have earned this,' he said, smiling loudly.

the drunken landlady - Reel

Tom and Eileen O'Neill (RIP) were the hosts of the legendary pub 'The House of McDonnell' in Ballycastle for many years. Theirs was a haven for traditional music and traditional musicians. Their welcomes are the stuff of legend. It was rare indeed for Eileen to 'let the hair down' but this piece celebrates one such event.

45 - sailing into walpole's marsh
(Trad title)

"Walpole maybe owns the land, he doesn't own the air.
Time we helped ourselves to the creatures found up
there."

Clumps of reeds in the marsh pointed at the moon,
"Those ducks upon their nests me boys, we shall visit
soon."

Three of them in waders pushed the boat from shore
and saw the stars upon the lake glistening by the score.

Not a sound the bow did make and as the oars fell
outlines in the fading light of targets them did tell.

"Lads prepare a banquet," said Johnny all at once
Shane stood up, fell right in, Tony yelled, "You dunce!"

The splash it tossed the feathers and upwardly they
flew,
Tony grabbed his shotgun and Johnny grabbed his too.

Shane pulled himself ashore some thirty yards away.
He heard the two boys blasting and to himself did say,

"They couldn't hit a cow's behind with an old banjo,"
the ducks flew into the night to where they did not
know.

Yonder in old Walpole's house a candle soon did burn
then another and another as the boat they tried to
turn.

They rowed and rowed in circles, a panic did result,
Shane took aim and hit both heads with his catapult.

"Hurry back and rescue me," he called out from the
mud.
They steered the little vessel toward him best they
could.

96

A hail of lead flew over them and in a twist of luck
Walpole's shot from the air to earth it brought a duck!

"Ha ha me boys," Tony cried, "We shall have a feast
and then come back tomorrow this time from the east."

They laughed until home they got after two a.m.
but if it's ducks you're after I wouldn't go with them!

sailing into walpole's marsh - reel

Another very poetic title here. I read that it was inspired by some duck poaching down in Kerry back in the day from a certain Ebenezer Walpole, the local landlord. Sure, you would hardly blame them for that.

46 - the kylebrack rambler
(Original title by Finbarr Dwyer RIP)

No more to ramble through columns of ash
nor trek upon the tumbling land
that sweeps to the shore, to sea and sand.
My kin and I now under the lash
of that cruel and wicked human hand.

My name is Mac Tíre and long have I been
patrolling these forests dense and dark.
Guardian of souls, of bush and of bark
of myth and of legend, heard and seen
is my future deemed, bleak and stark.

My howl now lost 'neath canon and gun,
the axes and saws slash near my lair
the thud of marching loud on the air,
I melt away like snow after sun
vanishing fast, the fools do not care.

Those that shared and shaped the ground
among their gods allowed me to walk.
And I contented often would talk
with travellers freely moving around
before for reward fate did me stalk.

When next you step the woods of Kylebrack
listen for me soft on the breeze.
I call from a past still amongst trees
and ask that you keep safe my pack
in dreams that even time cannot freeze.

the kylebrack rambler - reel

A fabulous tune, not for the fainthearted. It is as full of intrigue as the darkest forest no doubt. I thought that of all animals the wolf would ramble most and in Ireland for centuries this was the case. Alas the hand of man, yet again, ended his journey here.

47 - the lilting banshee
(Trad title)

The Ghostly Fleadh at Halloween
Is the weirdest fleadh ever seen.

Every year the dead arise
and try to win this music prize.

The range of entrants truly vast,
though best days behind are past.

Clearing dust out from throats,
still they sound like crazy goats.

Around the table sit the ghouls,
wailing on their wooden stools.

The song they sang, harsh and rough,
really was appalling stuff.

When they reached the final verse,
judges said, "Never worse!

You'll not win our talent show.
Now back down to hell you go."

On banjo next a zombie played,
left and right there it swayed.

It moaned along with every note,
the judges said, "Get your coat."

Off it moped seeking brains.
"It's just not fair," he complains.

"Next year will be mine I swear."
Then disappeared into thin air.

Came werewolves next in a pack,
each with bodhráns on their back.

The howling and the thumping then
made us think the world would end.

100

Judges at their notes looked down
Who would end this awful sound?

"Stop!" said one. "Rehearsals needed."
With foul looks his word they heeded.

Looking glum and feeling vexed
the judges dreaded who'd be next

till a banshee took her chair,
and began to lilt a rolling air.

She captured all with her voice
"Yes! At last. An easy choice.

The winner of the fleadh this year...
The Lilting Banshee," each did cheer.

the lilting banshee - jig

This is often one of the first tunes young trad musicians learn as they begin their journey. With that in mind I thought this piece would make a suitable partner for such a great tune.

48 - to the air of - the boys of bluehill
(Trad title)

As I was goin' down the road
without a care or a load
Didn't I happen on a crowd playing road bowls
Sure they said they were the best
never put to any test
And could beat any team by a margin of goals
Well I bein' one for fun
said, "'Tis time that we begun
To see if your claim it is substantial."
So I let them know me plan
that we'd match them man for man
With a prize that was sure to be financial

Well a date and time were set
the captains made the bet
Each team was permitted practice for a week.
At the road in Mullach Bán
on its sides the crowd did stand
silver bullets flew along their marks all to seek.
Jamesy raced to the line
his aim was rarely fine
the bowl like a rocket from his hand did go
but suddenly came a howl
his opponent shouted "Foul!
You hit me on the foot and I'm sure you broke my toe."

Shot for shot was matched
and from all around they watched,
such excitement in the parish never seen before
Till again an awful din
Colm was hit above the shin
The metal ball hit a bone, by God that was sore.
But on and on it went
Both teams were nearly spent
Only one shot each was left to satisfy the game
Tommy T wiped his brow
the time to strike was now
he windmilled his arm and tried victory to claim

Well it blasted through a shed
hit two spectators on the head
eventually stopping safe beneath the rusty gate
The other team were appalled
shouting that's not fair at all.
"If Tommy throws again the town will he'll decimate."
But up came Charlie Sloan
many's a bowl he'd thrown
His shirt was opened up halfway to his waist
His arm like a propeller
that was going interstellar
released his bowl (they say) at a hundred miles an hour

That was the winning blow
But their captain said. "You know,
It took all that we had to get the win today.
Sure the bet we'll split in two
come on we'll have a few
Biddy's is open now... well what do you say?
I spat upon my palm
and grabbed him by the hand
it would be an honour to hit the town with you
and so off both teams went
and the winnings they were spent
Drinking pints and songs, what else could we do?

A typical mid game scene...
The money has changed hands, the weather is with us, now bowl like the divil!
A great game most commonly played these days in Armagh and Cork and occasionally the Ryan Road!

the boys of bluehill - hornpipe

This is a very common hornpipe often associated with young musicians starting off. However, it's always a joy to hear it played no matter what age the player.

49 - the teetotaller
(Trad title)

Some days he'll stare at a glass, tasting
A memory. Often one without fanfare

Like a Tuesday during the forbidden
Hours of afternoon when he sat there

Steered in on a mad notion, a whim,
A turn into half light and familiarity.

"The usual?" Comes her voice on cue.
Ensues a yarn, a tall tale, hilarity

And the passing of time like a river.
Minutes would slide by in measures

Company would come and depart
Cognisant of Wednesday pressures.

Maybe it was a Thursday, not sure
When the sweetness diminished.

even the black lost its mystery
and when the last was finished

he started again nervously at first.
Until in these intervening years

A truce and well earned contentment
In mugs of tea and a yarn...cheers.

the teetotaller - reel

I think this tune, like some we've met already, has a second name, The Temperance. In either case this piece looks at the decision to stick with soft drinks.

50 - the bucks of oranmore
(Trad title)

Cillian and Fiachra, as close as close could be
Not really a surprise when you know the family

They built a magic treehouse in the corner of the yard
And getting into trouble they didn't find too hard

One day as they were peering out into the bay
They spied a skull and crossbones heading up their way

"Ahoy! Ahoy!" said Fiachra grabbing fast his blade
"Those devil's from north Antrim mean us to invade!"

"Well that's not going to happen," Cillian yelled aloud
Mounting there his stallion, shining, black and proud

Fiachra lifted high his sword his steed he gathered near
The brothers fast for the beach bravely then did steer

Underneath their shining boots crunching shells and stones
Matched their hearty yells, "We're gonna crush their bones."

"I hear onboard they have a thing some devil dark has made
No session in old Galway shall ever hear it played."

"It looks a little like a spoon and sounds like rusty tin
"Yes," said Cillian with a wink, "a most disastrous din."

Coming from the vessel and roaring from the deck
The captain said, "My banjo bright will every session wreck."

The twins agreed they'd have to act and jumped into a boat
And rowed like medal winners to quell each nasty note

They clambered quickly up the side and faced the captain foul
He plinked his e string harshly and then released a howl

It snapped just like a twiglet and flew straight up his nose
"No more reels for you," they laughed, "or polkas I suppose."

108

The captain cried, "Surrender' have mercy on me please."
"Take lessons on the fiddle and your punishment will ease."

He turned his boat and headed home his banjo on his knee
The twins high fived and laughed, "From banjos we are free!"

In victory to the treehouse the place they most adore
Returned the boys now known as the Bucks of Oranmore

the bucks of oranmore – reel

A great tune to finish off this collection. I dedicate this piece to two great young lads, Cillian and Fiachra and their parents Conor McCarthy and Yvonne Flynn all to be found in beautiful Oranmore, County Galway.

Also by Michael Sands.

Two books of poetry:

Away with Words

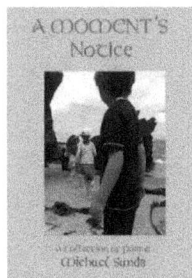

A Moment's Notice

A children's novel

Nut Hollow, The Knife and Nefairious

Also of interest

Donnchadh MacSuibhne
(Denis Sweeney) :

A Master's Collection

Compiled by Johnny Murphy

Clachan is a small, niche publishing company,
that specialises in short-run editions of
family and local histories, local interest publications, poetry,
and the like.
We also publish modern editions of antiquarian books.
These are carefully formatted and edited to modern
standards.
Our publications are available on our website: www.clachan-publishing.co.uk.

Clachan
Publishing

www.ingramcontent.com/pod-product-compliance
Lightning Source LLC
LaVergne TN
LVHW021130080426
835511LV00010B/1805